TORNADOES

BY PETER MURRAY

The Child's World

Published by The Child's World®
1980 Lookout Drive • Mankato, MN 56003-1705
800-599-READ • www.childsworld.com

ACKNOWLEDGMENTS
The Child's World®: Mary Berendes, Publishing Director
Olivia Gregory: Editing

PHOTO CREDITS
© bartuchna@yahoo.pl/Shutterstock.com: 13; Cheryl A. Meyer/
Shutterstock.com: 21; Dan Craggs via Wikimedia Commons: 11;
duallogic/BigStock.com: 10; Gino Santa Maria/BigStock.com: 15;
Ken Schulze/Shutterstock.com: 17; Lightningtodd/Dreamstime.com:
9; Minerva Studio/BigStock.com: 5; sdecoret/Shutterstock.com:
18; Twildlife/Dreamstime.com: 7

ISBN 9781631437687
LCCN 2014945421

Printed in the United States of America
Mankato, MN
November, 2014
PA02245

ABOUT THE AUTHOR

Peter Murray has written more than 80 children's books on science, nature, history, and other topics. He also writes novels for adults and teens under the name Pete Hautman. An animal lover, Peter lives in Golden Valley, Minnesota, in a house with one woman, two poodles, several dozen spiders, thousands of microscopic dust mites, and an occasional mouse.

Table of Contents

4   Tornado!

6   The Funnel Cloud

8   Slow or Fast Movers

11   Tornado Alley

12   Waterspouts

14   Dangerous Twisters

16   Lots of Damage

19   Staying Safe

22   Glossary

23   To Find Out More

24   Index

Tornado!

It is late in the afternoon on a hot summer day. The air is still and thick and moist. Tall, fluffy clouds appear in the sky. As they move toward you, you can see their dark undersides.

Over a few hours, the air cools and the sky takes on a strange, yellowish glow. A wind begins to blow, getting stronger every minute. Soon it whips your hair against your cheeks. A scrap of paper goes sailing up into the air. Tree branches bend, weeds tumble across the grass, and leaves fly through the air. Maybe it's time to take shelter! This could be tornado weather.

This huge storm is forming over a field in Texas.

The Funnel Cloud

Funnel clouds often form from cumulus (KYOO-myoo-lus) clouds.

Tornadoes can appear almost clear until they begin to suck up dirt and dust.

From the safety of your house, you watch the dark clouds. You see rain falling and a flash of lightning. Seconds later, you hear crackling thunder. The underside of the thundercloud bulges and twists around itself. The bulge begins to spin faster and faster. Soon a cone-like shape drops from the cloud. This shape is called a **funnel cloud**.

As the funnel cloud stretches downward, you hear a rushing sound. The tip of the funnel waves and dances above the ground. For a moment it looks as though it will return to the clouds.

Suddenly the tip drops down, touching the ground. A dark cloud boils up from the spinning cone. Dirt and dust are sucked into it, instantly turning the cone dark gray. You hear a sound like a freight train, getting louder and louder, coming right at you. The funnel cloud has become a tornado!

Here you can see a funnel cloud forming over a prairie.

Slow or Fast Movers

The average tornado speed is about 30 miles (48 km) per hour. But they can move up to about 70 miles (113 km) per hour.

Tornadoes usually happen between the hours of 3–9 P.M.

The Fujita Scale was created in 1971. Scientists updated the scale in 2007.

Since 1950, there have only been 58 EF5 tornadoes.

Some tornadoes last only a few seconds. Others last for hours. Tornadoes can spin in one place or travel faster than a car. When you see a tornado coming, there is only one smart thing to do—take shelter!

Scientists measure tornadoes with the **Fujita Scale**. This system measures wind speeds and looks at the damage a tornado causes. Scientists then rank the tornado from EF0 to EF5. A very weak, narrow tornado that causes little to no damage is measured at EF0. A wide, fast, powerful, and destructive tornado would be an EF5. EF5 tornadoes are very rare.

Enhanced Fujita Scale* *In use since 2007	
EF–0	65–85 mph winds
EF–1	86–110 mph
EF–2	111–135 mph
EF–3	136–165 mph
EF–4	166–200 mph
EF–5	> 200 mph

This dangerous storm produced a huge tornado and lots of hail.

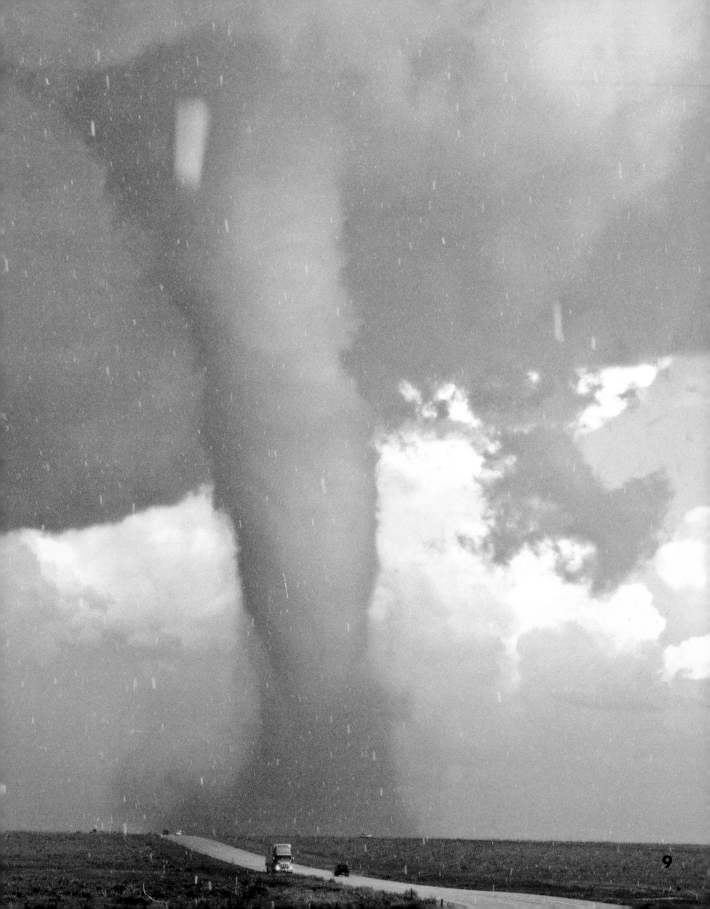

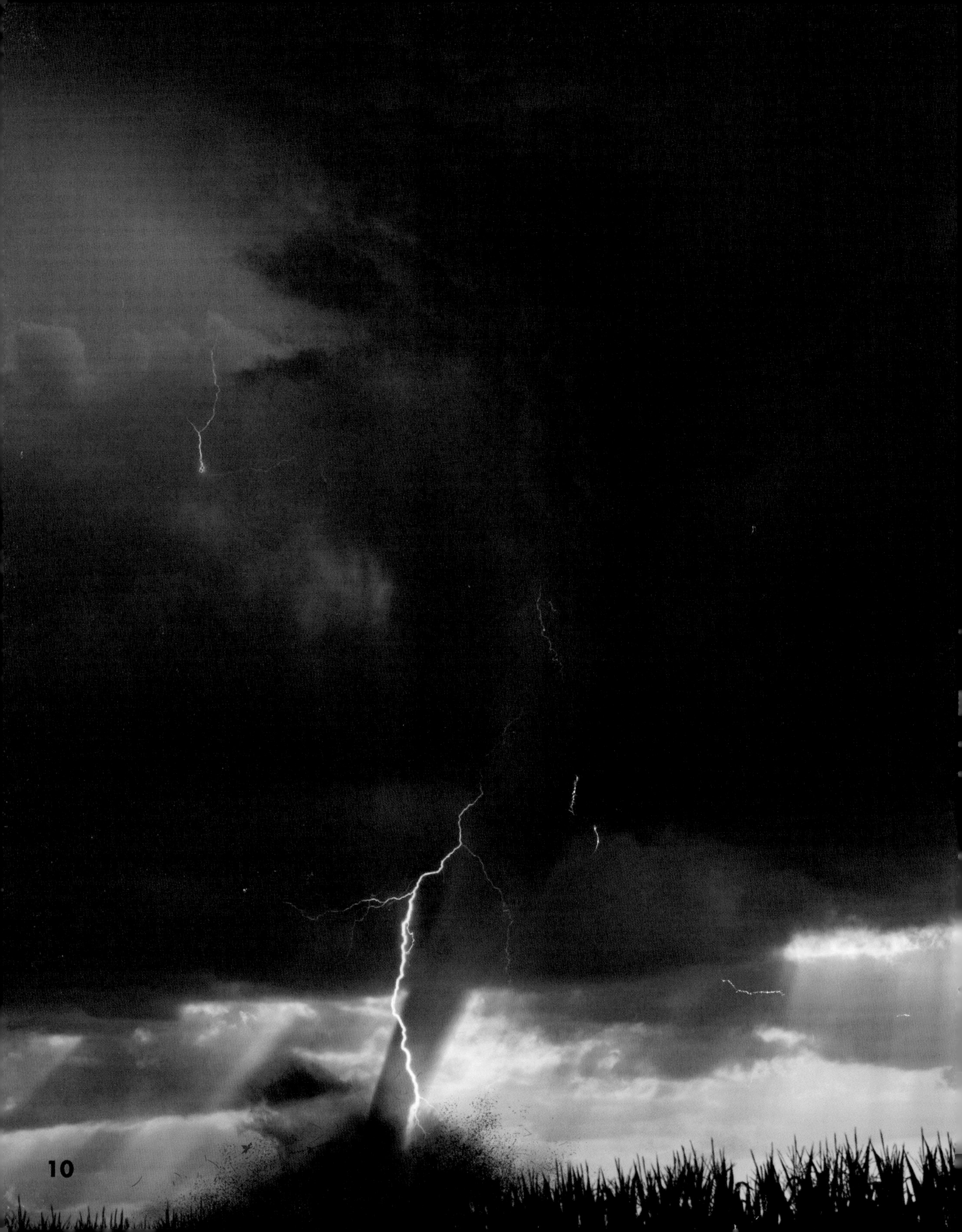

Tornado Alley

Hundreds of tornadoes touch down in North America's "Tornado Alley" every year. Tornado Alley includes most of the central United States, from Texas to Minnesota. In those areas, warm, moist air from the Gulf of Mexico meets cool, dry air from Canada. The air swirls around itself, creating powerful winds.

As the moist air rises high into the air, it packs tightly together, or **condenses**. The winds and moist air keep moving, forming towering thunderclouds. This is the perfect weather for thunderstorms. And wherever there are thunderstorms, tornadoes are possible.

The United States has about 1,200 tornadoes a year—more than any other country.

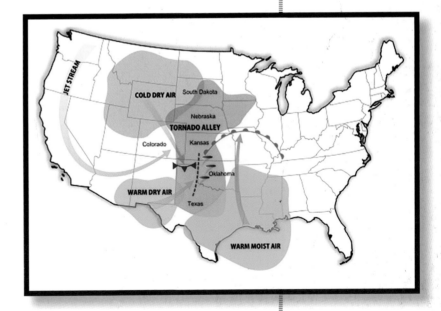

Tornadoes sometimes happen while there is sunny weather nearby.

Waterspouts

There are two types of waterspouts. "Tornadic" waterspouts occur over water. "Snowspouts" only happen when very cold air is present.

Waterspouts are very weak. They don't even suck up any water.

Tornadoes are most likely to happen in North America or Australia. But that doesn't mean they don't happen in other areas. In fact, tornadoes happen even in the middle of the ocean! When tornadoes form over water, they are called **waterspouts**.

Waterspouts like this one cause lots of water to swirl around at the bottom.

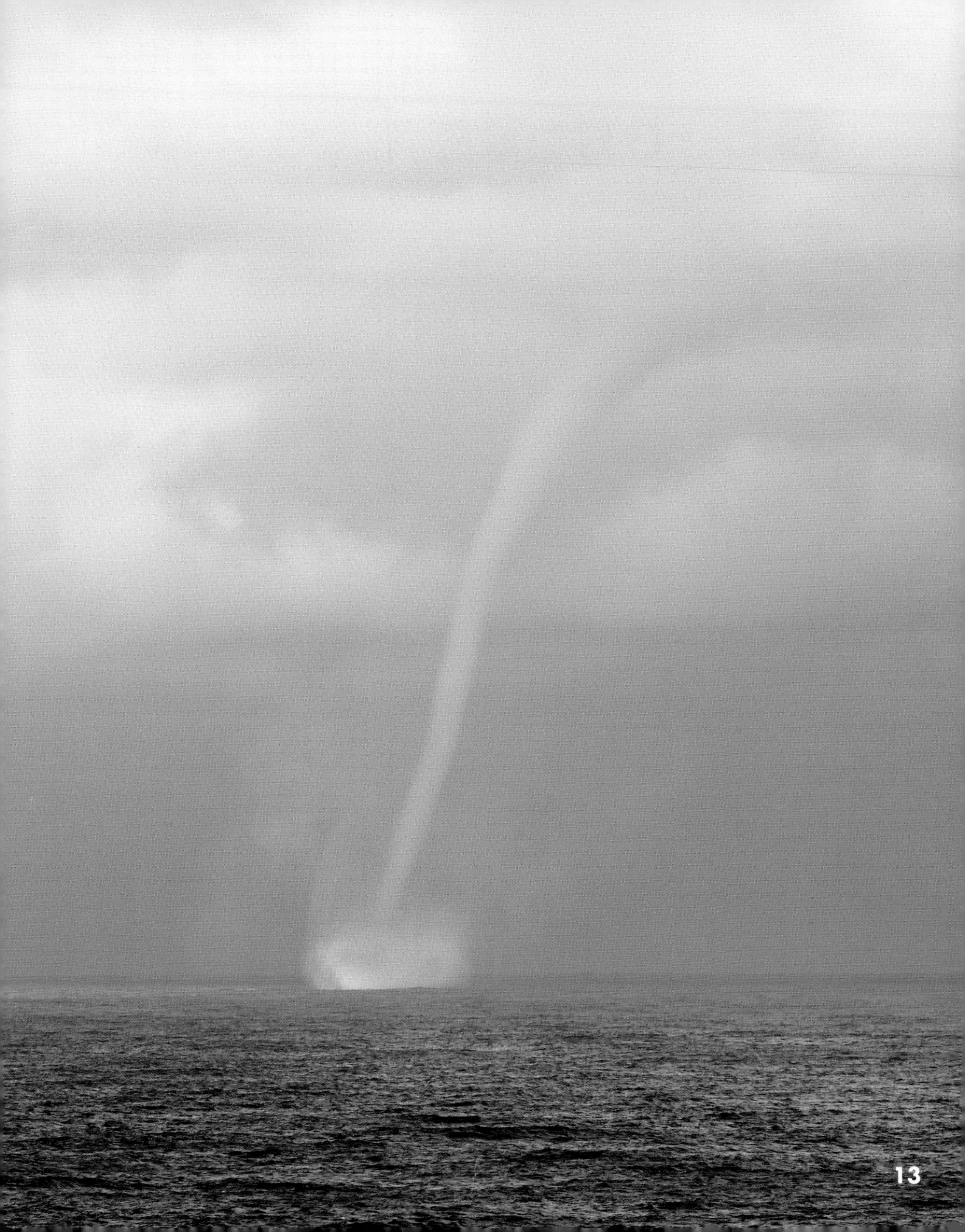

Dangerous Twisters

Most tornadoes do little damage. They touch down in open areas such as fields. They last only a few minutes, and then they disappear.

Other tornadoes are not so friendly. In 1965, six states were hit by a series of 37 tornadoes. The tornadoes caused 271 deaths. The worst tornado on record was the famous Tri-State Tornado of 1925. This giant tornado traveled 219 miles (352 km) through Missouri, Illinois, and Indiana. It killed 689 people and ruined 1,100 homes.

You can see the damage a 2011 tornado caused in Missouri.

Lots of Damage

Before the Fujita Scale, scientists could only guess at how fast a tornado's winds were by the amount of damage it caused.

EF0 tornadoes cause windows to break and branches to fall from trees. EF5 tornadoes tear homes from the ground and carry debris for miles.

Tornadoes produce the most powerful winds on Earth. In fact, a large tornado can create winds of up to 300 miles (483 km) per hour. That's strong enough to blow a railroad car off its track!

Tornadoes are also dangerous because of their spinning. A tornado's swirling winds create a **vacuum** inside the funnel. The vacuum can suck things in or blow them apart. When the funnel passes over a house, the vacuum and the winds can cause the house to explode. Sometimes the tornado's vacuum sucks up cars, trees, and even people.

A tornado in Illinois destroyed this house and a nearby tree.

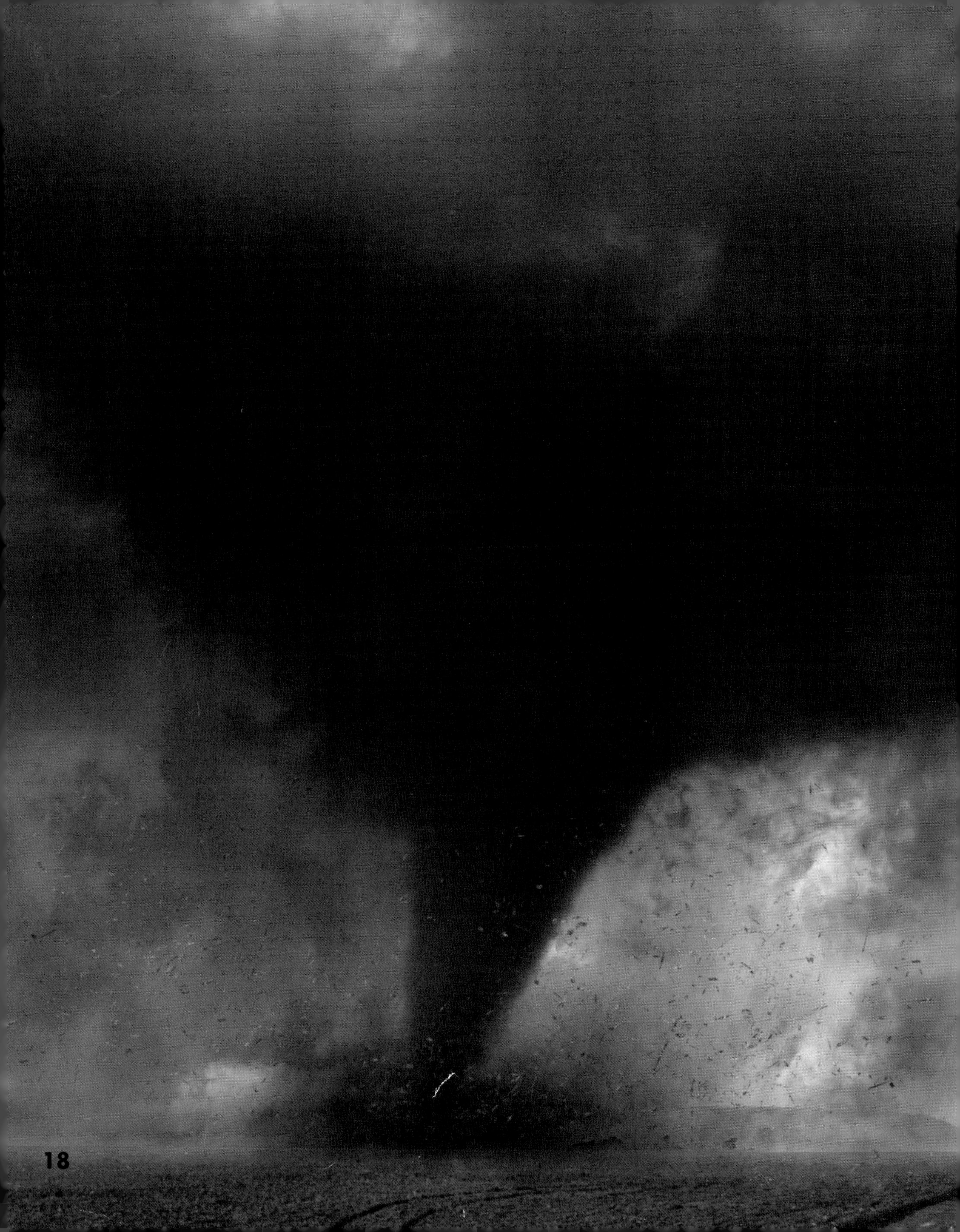

Staying Safe

Even if you live right in the middle of Tornado Alley, you might never see a twister. Only about one thunderstorm out of a thousand produces a tornado. Still, it's smart to be prepared. Knowing what to do in a tornado can save your life.

Never try to outrun a tornado in a car or on your bike. Even though they might look slow, tornadoes are very fast and can change directions quickly. And don't stay outside to watch! The safest place to be during a tornado is inside.

The states that get the most tornadoes are Florida, Oklahoma, Kansas, and Texas.

Tornadoes in the northern parts of the world spin counterclockwise. In the southern parts of the world, tornadoes spin clockwise.

This tornado is stirring up lots of leaves and dirt as it passes over a field.

You can make your own tornado safety kit. Fill a plastic bin with things such as a flashlight, a radio, batteries, blankets, some bottles of water, a can opener, and canned food.

At the first sign of a tornado, you should head for your house. If you have a basement or a storm cellar, that's where you should be. If you don't have a basement, hide in a closet or under a heavy table. And stay away from windows! Most people injured in tornadoes are hurt by falling objects or broken glass.

Today, scientists are trying to learn as much as they can about tornadoes. They study the winds and clouds of thunderstorms before tornadoes form. They also try to predict where each tornado will touch down. By learning more about tornadoes, scientists may one day be able to keep people safe from these powerful forces of nature.

Storm shelters are often clearly marked, like this one in Nebraska. Anyone can use them to stay safe.

Glossary

condenses (kon-DEN-sez)
When something condenses, it becomes tightly packed together. Moist air condenses in clouds to form rain and snow.

Fujita Scale (foo-JEE-tuh SKAYL)
The Fujita Scale is how scientists measure tornadoes. The measurements range from EF0 to EF5. The strongest tornadoes are EF5s.

funnel cloud (FUN-nul CLOWD)
A funnel cloud is a cone-shaped cloud in a storm. Many funnel clouds turn into tornadoes.

vacuum (VAK-yoom)
A vacuum can suck things in or blow them apart. Swirling winds inside a tornado's funnel create a vacuum.

waterspout (WA-tur-spowt)
A waterspout is a tornado that forms over water.

To Find Out More

In the Library

Challoner, Jack. *Hurricane & Tornado*. New York: DK Publishing, 2014.

Fradin, Judith Bloom, and Dennis B. Fradin. *Tornado! The Story Behind These Twisting, Turning, Spinning, and Spiraling Storms*. Washington, D.C.: National Geographic, 2011.

Gibbons, Gail. *Tornadoes!* New York: Holiday House, 2009.

On the Web

Visit our Web site for links about tornadoes:
www.childsworld.com/links

Note to Parents, Teachers, and Librarians: We routinely check our Web links to make sure they're safe, active sites—so encourage your readers to check them out!

Index

appearance, 6
Australia, 12

Canada, 11
color, 6
condenses, 11
cumulus clouds, 6

damage, 14, 16

EF5 tornadoes, 8, 14, 16

formation, 4, 6, 11
Fujita Scale, 8, 14, 16
funnel cloud, 6

Gulf of Mexico, 11

Illinois, 14, 16
Indiana, 14

Kansas, 19

Minnesota, 11
Missouri, 14

Nebraska, 20

Oklahoma, 19

shapes, 4, 6
snowspouts, 12
speed, 8, 19
staying safe, 19, 20

Texas, 4, 11, 19
Tornado Alley, 11, 19
Tri-State Tornado, 14
twisters, 4

vacuum, 16

waterspouts, 12
wind speeds, 8, 16